SITUATIONS

&

ISSUES

THE POETIC TRANSLATION

Vic Publication
CYICARE24U@YAHOO.COM
Michelle Clark Robertson/ FB
Copyright © 2015, Michelle Robertson 1st Edition
All Rights Reserved
ISBN- 13: 1515376583
ISBN- 10: 1515376583

Book Design by Craig Robertson

Acknowledgments

I want to give a special shout out to my sister Carolyn Clark. You are always on the front line of giving. Everybody can give (something) but not everybody knows how to give. I sit back and think of how blessed I am to be your sister. Thank you for being the wind beneath my wing.

To my husband Craig Robertson, my sister Lynn Leader and my friend Antione Torie Pittman; many people have shown support but the three of you have been faithful since the first stroke of the pen. The time you've taken to read my writing in spite of your own everyday tasks means a lot to me. The extra time you've put in to write reviews and tell others about my work is greatly appreciated.

Shout out and glory to God, for J. Cecilia, Kyrie, Khailel, Jayden.

To my children, grands, family and friends, thank you for the input each of you have in my life.

To you the readers, I write with a passion to fulfill your reading experience. Thank you for allowing me to entertain your time.

Finally, I have to dedicate praise to my God.

MY GOD

When I hear thunder at its loudest

When I see the rains pour

When rainbows grace the skies

Or stars shining in the mist of the sky's décor

I smile and say to myself

Surely He is King of kings and Lord of lords

But most of all He's

My God

When the rain pours and beat upon the house

I slowly praise His name, as I'm quiet as a mouse

When thunder boom shaking everything above ground

I'm startle in my movement but I embrace the sound

I'm at awe in my steps but I gently give a nod

As I quietly sit back and listen to the sounds of

My God

Introduction

Introduction is a form of romance,

A first impression leaving a mark or trance

Understood as the beginning of an engagement

As the formal steps for acknowledgement;

You either love them or leave them

Like them or not

Invite more conversation

Or anticipate the moment it'll stop.

My goal is to put you in a trance

While I make my mark

Give you a sample of my work from the start.

For I have taken subjects and formulate rhythm for what's being read or heard,

And designed it as a creative style of language called

Spoken Words.

A WOMAN SCORNED

Her voice will be heard, even when her attitude is not popping;

Rather loud or quietly spoken

To her there's no stopping.

She's not to be played with

She's not to be dared

And even on her best of days, her agenda is to be feared.

She's broken without shame, for her brokenness is the norm.

For her everyone is the same, no one can be transformed.

Her pain runs deep, behind her painted smiles.

She's just as dangerous as a snake, even when she's sweet as a child.

It would be a deadly error to take her kindness for weakness;

Because for her, love is shallow and she sees revenge as meekness.

Her definition of love is dark, unclaimed and unfulfilled.

Dreams don't exist, they're everything but real.

Trace her tears if you can get close enough; And follow them to a chamber that is actually filled with love.

With closed openings, and windows that are sealed; lost keys and doors made of steel;

She makes love to toxic memories; she embraces its pain.

Her conscience is impermeable, wrapping her heart in chains.

She's held captive, while slowly dying inside; preventing entry of any kind.

For unlike a heart that's worn, a heart that's torn; is nothing less than a woman scorned.

THAT'S HIM

He enters the room and sashay in the opposite direction, taking my next breath with him.

Others cross his path, blocking my view and in my heart I cursed them.

Anxiety overtake me when I catch my breath, he's like a medicine my body needs.

He reappears and calms my fear; once again my eyes are pleased.

A certain rush to feel his touch spark my audacity;

To draw him near with a look not quite a stare for that is my specialty.

Just last night as I dreamt of being held in his arms, I looked up in his face;

Calculated every trace;

His charcoal eyes,

His full lips,

His dark complexion base;

That's how I know that's Him.

He makes love like a liberator.

His kisses are like the breath of life.

His arms are an incubator, separating wrong from right.

As he slowly approaches, I can't help but notice,

How right the moment feels;

My heart dance with his eyes, my eyes dance with his steps,

He's no longer near but here.

Face to face, doubt never had a chance;

My imaginations, my dreams and every vision I had, made disbelief impossible or slim.

They are my witness, that's him.

I pick up my glass, for him I give a toast;

The bartender smiles because he already knows;

As he refills my glass all the way to the rim;

The last one of many of them… that's him.

THE MOMENT

She gave him life but it cut like a knife.

What was given to him was taken from her;

The precious moment she'd been waiting for.

For him the door will open, for her the door will close.

One shall go forth, while the other goes cold.

He will make his mark while her mark gently fades away.

One will rise up, while the other one lay.

A set of eyes will close, yet another set will open wide.

One enters the picture while the other subsides.

They once had the same heartbeat; they once took the same breath.

They once shared the future; they once battle life protests.

Yet in passing, time will not allow them to meet.

One will inhale the breath of conquer; the other will exhale life's defeat.

But at this moment they both are precious;

At this moment they both are as delicate as flowers.

A match made in heaven, yet their fate one dare not desirer.

The Moment was written in memory of women who've died giving birth. A time that is supposed to be joyful and anticipated have in some cases been bitter sweet and left unspoken of.

EMPTY HEART

An irregular heartbeat barely makes a sound,

Void of adequate blood flow,

Communication it does not know,

Interaction is a no-no

For its emotions exist solo.

With passions being disconnected

And forgiveness being absent,

Darkness is always present

It's frame a deadly capsule.

Sin hibernates in its wall.

The devil looks at it and is flatter.

Love isn't a resident;

And the sweetest of melody is as a clatter.

Intimacy is an intrusion, failing at its best.

Affection has no desires or purpose, annulled of fulfilling any request.

The empty heart forfeits entry of any kind of positive flow;

It drowns in its own darkness and insists on its own bravo.

Hidden behind flesh that screams for the breath of life;

An empty heart is just that...empty.

Empty....of anything other than strife.

LET GO OF YOU

I was riding on faith while you were riding on luck.

I chose to trust while you chose to mess up.

I held my position, hoping you would come around;

But your last blow to my heart caused a sister to shut down.

The disappointments from expectations and the echo of all your lies,

Lost all of its power the last time I cried.

I will now let go and move on with my life;

You can keep your aggravations, heartaches and unnecessary fights.

I decided the best thing I could do.... is let go of you.

Let go of you! ...Yes, let go of you.

I figure it out, with the so many things left unsaid, that the words that were spoken were so that I might be misled.

Now that which was done in the dark has come to the light.

Because you forgot it's God that fights my battles and I stand in the armor of His might.

So while you were tearing me down, God was building me up;

I have not just what I need, I have more than enough.

And in spite of everything you choose to do,

It doesn't change the fact, I'm letting go of you.

ORGASM   *(Just a funny way of looking at things)*

Nothing is like being well fed and you enjoyed the meal.

Imagine being completely sedative without the help of a pill.

Receiving a tax refund and you holler, because you got more than you thought you would get.

Finding a dress that compliments every curve of your body, having the perfect fit;

Being set free after being held hostage;

Creating a motion picture, in which the creativity is non-stopping.

Letting go and receiving everything you ever wanted in return.

It's like walking through fire and not being burn.

It's like hitting the lottery in all 50 states; you awake to find it's just a dream;

But it still feels real when you awake; although nothing around you have changed.

And all the turmoil within you complies as advised... until again the need arise.

Your senses are now on full alert; your body revitalized.

A GODLY MAN

It's good that he can pray it's expected of a godly man; going to church on a regular and taking a positive stand.

However, I need to know can he weather the storm, stand by my side and remain spiritually strong.

Walk away from temptation when it involves sexual sin, be a standard of light against promiscuous trends.

Represent in character rather he's around friends or strangers; in the most secrets of places; in the most appealing of dangers.

Speak with integrity, have a sense of but is not govern by pride. He's able to instruct in counsel because he is known to be wise.

Like Samson... defends in danger, assures in fear, stands in struggles, in his absence remain near.

Like Joseph ...he finds his purpose worth the investment and does whatever is necessary for it to be.

Like Moses...handled his affairs like a man of God, so his family can trust him to lead.

He does his business with a grateful heart being thankful he's able to provide.

Walk with a purpose, knows who he is and refuses to live a lie.

He's trustworthy and leads unselfishly; godly wisdom he always seeks.

Being mindful of his temper both physically and verbally; avoids using foul language as a regular form of speech.

He's remains a picture of strength even when he's lost all his might.

A knight and shining armor for his children;

A ray of beacon for his wife,

But most of all he's not just a man

He's a man with an honorable quality of life.

THE SCRAPS

Looking way-way back, history type of long time ago;

When we lost everything from our freedom, to our bodies, suppressed under forbidden control;

We were given little as possible yet expected to give more in return.

Our future was dark and uncertain, yet through it all we still learned.

Leftover food called scraps, often kept our families well fed.

If it wasn't for the scraps we all would be dead.

Dressing that is sometimes called stuffing was a combination of season breads and meats;

A mixture of the very foods thrown out not fit to keep;

Their shoes if any were worn; never given to them new;

Had the sole of cardboard boxes; the scraps, that got them through.

They were covered by scraps of clothing, gathered and reused when can;

Handed from hand to hand ... Often from bodies of dead men.

The scraps of denied education didn't allow them to learn or teach;

But they communicated through spiritual songs which gave them freedom of speech.

Living on scraps from a penny to a dime;

I doubt if some of them ever seen a dollar in their time.

It was the scraps of old buildings destine to cave in;

That housed our great Father's and Mother's, in conditions nothing less than sin.

While countless tears fell from their eyes and their hearts filled with fear;

The scraps of faith that they had, help them to persevere.

The scraps of laws called the Human Rights,

Govern their mistreatment; hunted them down in the nights.

The scraps of memories of ungodly, harsh and cruel hate;

Are the pictures of our history, in what's left to be trace.

So keep your scraps, they represent the struggles of pieces that were once whole.

Waiting to be reused, waiting for their stories to be told.

Stop despising your short comings, your disappointments, or shame

There's more to your struggle you have yet to gain.

Pick up the pieces and continue your journey of life

For you were never promise a bed or roses, but it's a guarantee you'll have to fight

Never doubt your abilities

Never sleep on your dreams

Never take life for granted

And remember things aren't always what it seems

There are poor men that were once rich and rich men that were once poor

Each having scraps of life that is worth more than gold

YOU NEED A RECEIPT

You're looking at me like I'm the one who cheats.

You wasted years of my life now you want a receipt!

There was no refund on the love I distribute.

No rebates on the time I waited for the love I shared, always an issue.

Love ran out and your check bounced;

So just sign the dotted lines to make sure you get your discount.

Everything is on your copy of the statement, no need for a receipt;

You withdrew more than you deposit, so don't be astonish by the interest rate.

You chose the streets,

Failing to invest in stock that held a real bond;

Now you're adding pennies instead of dollars and want me to check the sum.

You added when you should have subtracted, because you never check the records;

Trade-ins, called tricks, don't earn a profit if your product isn't worth the investment.

So this settlement serves as a form, of a lesson you need not to repeat.

Subtract whatever you have left... and oh yeah, you can keep the receipt.

THE SPIRITUAL INVASION

There is a spirit of antichrist creeping into the hearts of men;

Presenting itself as wisdom, in the form of new knowledge to comprehend;

Now people are questioning and mocking the things Christ did.

Picking and twisting the things He said.

They deny the fact He was born of a virgin;

They doubt He died and rose again.

This spirit is in the shadows of what they teach;

In the middle of testimonies when they speak.

Dancing with their emotions;

Distorting what they believe.

Whispering in their ears;

Changing the way they pray.

Perverting the image God planned out for man,

Giving immoralities fancy names, as if that makes it no longer a sin;

Relating to other gods in respect to our own,

Forgetting He is a zealous God and He is God alone.

Treating saying "I'm sorry" the same as "I repent."

Discrediting the Bible because it has different translations in print:

Challenging God's ability to still hold man accountable,

Ignoring such calibrated lies that the devil is telling us.

Passing laws that reflect the hearts of man instead of God;

Slowly, eliminating our rights for us to be set apart.

There is a spiritual invasion.

Warning, please be on alert.

It started on the outside but now it's entered the church.

EAU MEMORY

I walked into the room and looked into the, many his' and hers face.

Many in which hope left no trace.

Sound of anger, being put on file, filled the air,

Muffled by the cries to know, "Is there's anyone who cares."

The fear of the unknown, challenged my peace,

And I found comfort in knowing many traveled this road ahead of me.

So, I stood in what I called The Line of Mercy, when one must lay his pride aside;

And sought the care that I needed from another in order to be able to survive.

I met those who looked down on me.

I met many in my shoes.

I remember most; however, those who did what they could BEFORE saying I'll be praying for you.

The look on my children's faces, asked many questions.

So many questions, all at one time; And there I stood with so many of my own...God knows, while walking a thin line.

Here I am in my health and strength,

I'm not mentally ill and I'm physically fit.

Yet, I stand here in such a funky disposition,

All because of a budget cut made by some rich politician.

Empowered by determination,

Yet stagnated by circumstance;

My hope is in God, who has the blueprint of my life in His hand.

I've come a long ways since then, no longer homeless and standing in the welfare lines.

Yet, memories and the provoking feelings of the EAU often cross my mind.

When the Truth Sets In

Are you looking back or are you looking ahead?

Are you making excuses or the necessary changes instead?

Is there a finger pointing at everyone else,

To keep from turning the mirror on yourself?

Is there anger, attitude or any contention

Hidden issues you fail to confront yet along mention?

In light of all things, my brothers there are times when:

The jungle boogie has to stop and the truth sets in.

No matter how high the waves,

Some bridges must be cross.

One must know when to fight;

Verses surrendering and learning from the lost.

Choices have to be made.

Decisions must be face.

Consequences endure

And wounded faith reassured.

Holding on versus letting go;

Speaking up, versus saying no more…

Walking on versus standing still,

When the truth sets in, my sister, that's when life gets real.

You're in the sea of life…you either drown or swim.

So get understanding because without it knowledge is dim.

Obtain wisdom it is God's protection in life and always face the truth, to avoid living a lie.

The Family She Power

There are some people who are born to impress; impact and achieve;

The things impossible to encourage others to believe

You are that soul, to the different lives you've touched;

You're the glue that bonds our family.

You're our adrenaline rush.

You are the wind beneath our wings, the reflection of who we are;

You're not just another woman, you're our shining star.

Although age has often crippled you and time hasn't always been your friend,

You've handled life well and proven your strength time and time again.

Your torch who, will carry when your light is low?

How will we say good-bye, when we have to let you go?

A bona-fide woman, few will ever duplicate;

So we acknowledge your presence, as we embrace your traits.

You have marked our family as a spiritual monument.

You are our "she power"... undeniable relentless.

Death's Arrival

It's a moment in time that cannot be avoided.

No matter the flight or the arrival of its time,

Death has a way of hitting home,

 In a way that only the heart can define.

Rather unexpected or knowing of its approach,

It doesn't ease the pain of having to let go.

It's the exit of life; a path we all must take;

And every day we live, subconsciously for it we await.

DON'T BE JUST ANOTHER DREAM

Don't tell me you love me,

And really don't care.

Don't say what's in your heart,

When its' really not there.

Don't take away my hurt and give me more pain.

Don't be just another dream.

ACHING

My heart is aching for someone to love.

My mind is aching for someone to think of.

My feet are aching for someone to run to.

My mouth is aching for someone to confess "I love You."

My arms are aching for someone to hold.

My body is aching for someone to call my own.

My lips are aching for someone to kiss.

My dreams are aching for someone who exists.

HIDE AND SEEK HISTORY

Babies taken from their mothers arms,

Husbands and sons beaten until they bled,

Wives and daughters raped,

Young and old being shot down while they fled.

Unrecorded history blotted out the stories untold;

But if you listen close, you can hear the restless souls.

Generation after generation I came,

Raised up to think my color was a reason for shame.

Cripple by the laws of the land;

Because their verdict ruled I was less than a human.

I've been viciously abused, beaten until my skin pealed;

Treated like an animal and expected to still live.

I've cleaned and kept houses in which I could not lay my head.

Prepared and served meals that my family was never fed.

Now my blood cries out as you read and recollect "man! ... woman!... Do you see me?"

Dripping from branches,

Sliding down trees;

My blood poured out more than a thousand ways,

Yet I'm not in your history.

You don't talk about how my dark skin being the color of your child's first love,

Because our women breast where the ones that fed them until their hungry stomachs had enough.

Men rape our women when they had wives of their own,

Lay with them and made babies, both daughters and sons.

In shacks fit for a nigger they would often say,

But it was there that they would often sneak to lay.

Ignoring their scream and the eyes that accused, "You wanted her, "She didn't want you!"

Yes, I remember. I can relate.

It's the reason my soul can't rest and I'm wide awake.

My soul cries out when the sun is as hot as it can get;

When the rain is pouring, when other men are at rest;

When the lightening flashing and the thunder roar,

When snow is falling or it is icy cold.

Yes it is I, the voice that stirs one to talk about their shameful hate.

For when you are asleep, you I will awake.

It's like a game... they hide and you seek;

To discover the part of hidden history

We didn't have rights, so why did they cover their heads?

Burned our houses in the night,

Leave their wives to defile our beds:

Because their wickedness ran deep and cover them with shame;

They knew they were wrong but wouldn't accept the blame.

They were less than men in comparison to their slaves.

No integrity, lacking strength and carrying their self- hatred to the grave.

The truth is when they hung us from a tree,

We looked down on them and cursed their seed.

The one's who helped us to preserve our lives,

Were ridiculed and punished for doing what was right.

They would brag about our bodies hanging from a tree.

Ignore our blood when poured out in the streets.

Commit crimes and put it on a black man.

Amused themselves while watching us build the land.

They demonstrated hatred and passed it around like food.

And spread it to their children like callous fools.

But we don't talk about the time when they were the thugs.

Selling and trading men and women like they were gods.

The time when they were vile and dangerous to other men;

The senseless acts they committed and the laws they were allowed to bend.

The number of people they hurt

Ruthless and ungodly without a desire to change;

Doing nothing to eliminate the hate or get past their shame.

To hear this would anger him, he rather it be hid.

Unspoken of and forgotten, most certainly not written or read.

You don't know how we ourselves had babies by the masters; no one speak of those days

And had to get up out our beds and delivered the ones where he laid.

With two children born so close and us having to nurse two homes;

We would switch them out and have them raised the half black child as their own.

They were so color struck they could not see;

The child was half him and half me.

No, history doesn't talk about the vile mixture that would often end up on their plates;

After selling our children and taking our spouses away.

Or the coins we saved in spite of our situation

Held on to for years to set one free after several generations

The true value of a black man would eliminate the negative theories

Had they kept a record of all that we build, created and invented throughout history

The black men were appealing, authentic and strong

Uneducated yet still wise, America's real back bone.

So seek you that which is hidden.

Know the purpose of why it wasn't written.

Find the answers in the scramble memories of the old.

Hold on to the bits and pieces as one would gold.

Write them down and pass them on

There's more to the picture than what text books have drawn.

Frame the memoirs of letters, dairies, pictures and such

For they are our historical clutch

The chronological transition of the changes that may or may not have occurred

Our road map of footprints comparing facts against what we've heard.

Hidden events of people, places and things

Of our uncrown black queens and kings

Never given the respect and honor to them due

Still hidden, denied and waiting in lieu of the truth.

A WINDOW

A motion picture in a frame current with time itself;

Live within its frame; unable to be put on a shelf.

Its translucent shield divides reality while allowing one the view;

Of a transparent vision in sync with what's happening around you

Its custom limitations are designed to allow you to see out or in

Physically as a means of comfort

Mentally as a means to comprehend

To allow you to take notice of what's in front of you;

In order to deal with the present concerns of your current point of view:

Sealed windows make you aware but isolate

Cracked or broken windows obstruct your intake

Rather a window of opportunity or a window of escape;

The eye of the soul window or a window that usher night and day

With the option of opening or closing,

Or the ability to let in or out

It gives one the ability to just observed or psychologically reroute.

So when you stand at the window; you'll see several things but be mindful of two.

The revelation that is in your head and your physical point of view:

The interpretation of your findings along with what you now know

Makes looking through windows, prepare you for walking through doors.

The Next Exit

After toning down the massive tempo of life

I finally decided to take a different direction.

The way I was going didn't offer adequate protection.

Reducing my speed permitted me to yield

In order to buckle up, recuperate and heal.

The transportation of emotional turmoil's was like mental wrecks and traffic jams;

In opposition to where I want to be verses where I am.

I ignored the signs along the way, that said U-turn, road block straight ahead;

Turned a deaf ear to the warning sounds and the flashing lights of red;

I failed to take notice of the road construction in his life that was taking place;

And tried to travel a one-way street, to my own detriment, the wrong way.

A detour would have saved me but then again I'm not sure;
I was so in love with this man you couldn't tell me I wasn't secure.

I even kept on going after he handed me the brochure.

When the right lane closed, I should have come to a full stop.

But I never heed the warnings until my doctor stood before me like a stage prop.

Now I've gone from a brochure, to a ticket in my hand,

I passed every exit, now I've had come to a dead end.

When my doctor read me my rights, he said there was no cure.

Now I'm traveling down the roads looking back, as if I'm taking a tour.

The worst part of all is for a long time I was celibate;

And when I did decide to drive I took the wrong exit.

So if you are out there traveling; slow down and keep this in mind.

The streets are not going anywhere; when you do exit take your time

(In memory of a patient that use to always tell me, "Mrs. Michelle I lived life too fast.")

The Awe Hell List

It's the list of moments when you just want to turn the other way

When you're at a loss of words to say

When you can't believe what just happen

Someone did or said something and it's about to be some scrapping

When you've gotten caught doing something you didn't have any business

A situation just went down and you are an eye-witness

You're about to get laid with your man and he can't get up "Johnny"

When you need it the most someone steals your last li bit of money

You're late for work and the car won't start

A person of interest use to be your best friend sweetheart

You're in a position and the only way out is to run

You're watching the game and the other team won

A random one nightstand tells you she's having your baby

The person you were dating turns out to be crazy

You're eating something and it has a bug

You're dating someone and their unknown spouse shows up

The "Awe Hell" list is a crime shame

Because whatever happens nine times out of ten you can't change.

HOLLA AT ME

If your attitude is right and your time isn't tight

Holla at me

If you're ok with where you're at and you don't view troubles as a threat,

Holla at me

If your money doesn't make you and the man in the mirror isn't a fake, you.

Holla at me

If you can admit when you're wrong or forgive and move on,

Holla at me

But if you are none of these to say the least, don't even bother I rather keep the peace.

A WOMAN INTUITION

Your girl knew I was a woman too.

She should have told you I'll be hip to you.

Your changing ways, your smell, your moods and the lies,

She should have told you I would realize.

You told me lies and thought that I believed,

Everything that you said to me;

I wasn't sleep while you cheated, creeped and sneaked

I actually, knew you better than you did to say the least.

There was a difference from your strive to your sleep

Sealing the deal in the way you started handling me.

The only person that was really in the dark, was the character playing the main part.

The star, the main man, the brother with all the cards; in his hands

When you get a chance, you might want to look back over your plans

I too have a new dance.

WHAT TIME IS IT

What time is it? I can no longer tell.

It's hard to keep track of time when you're fighting like hell.

We're not throwing physical punches but we're in a fight,

To be heard... be acknowledge... to be entitled to our rights.

It doesn't seem we can cry loud enough... long enough.... Or hard enough to be heard:

And the idea of this working out peacefully is starting to seem absurd.

There are invisible boundaries that prohibit the rights of certain race.

Known evidence and facts disregarded right in our face.

Out rights violence with the whole world watching;

Division within our nation because our system level of humanity is dropping.

Setting an emotional condition in the mindset of a black man,

Forgetting that in a matter of time you will eventually cause him to play his own hand.

Where's the honor in a system, that fail to protect you from their own?

If I didn't know any better, I would think it was a systematic KKK clone.

With more children born interracial having the choice of multiple race

What will we tell them to prepare them for the ungodly debate?

I refuse to past along the hate

Created by the foolish heart that embraces sin

Because I know that there's good and bad in every race

Such judgment should not be based on one's skin.

For many hide and impersonate what's in their heart and how they feel

But their actions show plain and clear the hatred being conceals.

So what time is it? It's time for change. Eliminate hatred this country forefathers prearranged.

JUST A MOMENT AGO

Not even yesterday but just a moment ago,

I had the option of calling you on the phone

Hope of us crossing the same path

The idea of us seeing each other again.

I had no doubt I'll see someone we both knew

And they'll tell me that they just seen you.

Not just yesterday but just a moment ago.

We had the option of taking pictures you and I

The alternative of engaging in real talk or just shooting lies.

The choice of seeing each other later when it was convenient,

But I didn't see this coming;

Even now I don't know what the next few minutes are bringing.

Not just yesterday but just a moment ago,

You were "Just Here"

A second ago... just the other minute

An hour ago... just yesterday

The other week... last month... last year

They say, time flies but when it stops it locks;

And I wasn't ready for the break.

Wasn't ready for the discontinued, wasn't ready for this place.

Not just yesterday but just a moment ago.

I thought I could get to you if need be

Thought our goodbyes would always end with handshakes, hugs, kisses and "Peace."

I never gave thought to my heart breaking

And the tears that would fall

Or having to look back over my life to remember the last time we talk.

Not just yesterday but just a moment ago.

(In memory of my brother from another mother... Richard Bernard Super)

DADDY DOPE

I'm an unfathomable desirer

I can make you high

Rescue you from boredom... make you believe a lie.

I represent chemicals

That awake more than your body chemistry;

I'll make you kill, steal, beg, sell your soul short for me.

I can make you sweat when it's cold as ice,

Yet, I can make you cold as ice under a biopsy knife.

I possess the power...

To make you neglect your children

Rob your own home

Take someone's life... Including your own;

Forsake your God

And make you act a fool

For I am your master and you are my tool

I can become one's life and in some cases the cause of death.

I can take the wealthiest of man wealth.

I don't discriminate I take them young and old;

I even have clientele still in the womb.

I'm ready 24-7, any hour

I'm Daddy Dope

Don't doubt my power.

FROM THE BEGINNING WITHIN

At the time of conception; in God's mind I came to be.
And when He stretched out and died on the cross for you,
He was doing it also for the unseen me.

There's not nothing to figure out and one need not assume,
He clearly states I exist before I was even formed in the womb.

I don't need a face to face appearance

No need for me to be presently on the scene

Undeveloped and small as a seed... I'm still a human being.

If I'm not a human being, leave me alone and let me be

But that is not the case, because you're able to detect me, shortly
after I'm conceived.

So, the shenanigans that are used to discredit my right to life

Is like a married man saying he don't have a wife

It's like saying because you don't see the wind it don't exist

Or when a child is not physically with his or her mother or father
they're no longer parents

I have nowhere to flee, this is my plea

Don't make medical arrangement for some procedure to be the
death of me

It's all a lie; don't make death a tool or the rule

Give me life when you choose.

For there is a Ruler of the laws and orders of things decree

And He's already sets the regulations of what will and won't be;

He alone is God, without the laws of man.

He doesn't need you to vote it, regulate it or constitute it in.

If He says it's wrong, it is a sin.

And if He says its right, it doesn't need to be validated by man.

Because this is a touchy subject, I just want to say it is not to condemn or pass judgement in any way. It's a point of awareness for what I believe. At one time abortion was a very popular choice among women. It offered a way out of uncomfortable situations that allowed one to believe they were correcting a mistake. So if this is an experience you have had, remember you are in a different place now. Rather better or worst what's done is done. Learn from your experience and remember the choice is yours. We won't always agree; neither will we always walk hand in hand in the same direction in life.

SETTING BOUNDARIES ON MY PAST

I won't call everything I've ever done and regretted a mistake

Because somethings I did because I didn't like what was on my plate

Some things were done when I was young, dumb and having fun.

Then there were times when I ignored my inner voice;

Because I was afraid I didn't have much choice.

Life don't allow you to see your future through a glass,

So I've made mistakes and now I'm setting boundaries on my past.

I forgive myself for the things I did and cannot change.

If I could do it all again things defiantly wouldn't be the same.

Now, not all the choices I made produce negative results;

But we have a tendency to see things differently as we become older adults.

So I'm giving an account of where I've been and where I want to go.

I have to set boundaries on my past.

I have to open and close some doors.

I will allow myself to heal from wounds

Delete lies and toxic mental fumes.

Yes, I shall rise again, because I'm putting boundaries on my past.

If I don't it will destroy my plans.

I will speak aloud; no longer whisper out of shame

Point fingers at others or allow myself to be blame.

I understand we truly parish when we lack knowledge

And getting an understanding of life is better than getting a degree from college.

So it's not an issue or a matter of regret;

I'm just moving on and I'm setting boundaries on my past.

HIS HANDS

Compromise and silent years of tears
Procrastination to avoid dealing with the fears
The bearing thoughts of mental strong holds and mindsets,
It's your life in his hands I need you to project.

His hands have become like fire
And his words enhances its flames
His eyes mirror their danger
While your eyes mirror their pain.
His hands that you entrusted to make you feel loved and secure,
Promotes wounds of agony which he expects you to endure;

Now your crush at the presence of him:
His footsteps...
His smell...
His voice...
This man... His... His hands... His hands
Wake Up! Wake up Baby Girl!
He dag near kill you again.

Listen, registration is not required for you to take a stand,
And you can no longer seek mercy from this man's hands.
For they have formed as a weapon against you,
That could one day put you six feet under.
But what God has put together (That's you Baby Girl) let no man
put asunder.
Manage your emotions; make a decision to restore your health;
The battle with this brother belongs to the Lord,

You need to save yourself.
Should we partake to a phone call or maybe even a newsflash?
To find that you're no longer in the land of the living
And now we got this battle of un-forgiveness!

And what is there to be said if you're unable to recuperate?
And Lord have mercy should your help come too late.

Wake Up! Wake Up!
From the captivity of his hands
Wake Up! Wake Up!
This may be your last chance.
Wake Up! Wake Up!
My daughter... My sister... My mother... My friend.

Pt 2 HIS HANDS (Victim)

I will be the voice from the grave, the symbol of hope
Defeating the feelings of shame,
I will remember the lives taken and express the need for change.
I will cross this bridge and then extend my hand to another that
may have it to cross.
I will be that voice from the grave, of those whom we've already
lost.

I will stand as a lighthouse in darkness, to help show someone
else the way.
I will shout it out furiously, until I awake them from "A could be
grave."
I will face the truth and accept responsibility on my part.
I will walk away from the toxic, escaping from his heart.

I will approach my journey ahead mindful of what I've learned.
Focus on the changes I've made, being careful not to repeat or
return.
I will exchange what was a disposition, to a position of strength
and power.
And never again put myself in the hands of an abusive coward.

I stand at war against lethal relationships, warning those who
remain in it at will;
Not to underestimate domestic violence, for it not only destroys
and kills.

Wake Up! Wake Up!
From the captivity of his hands.
Wake Up! Wake Up!
This may be your last chance.
My daughter... My sister... My mother... My friend.

CROSSWORDS

Dubious ideologies said to make one believe one way, but really meaning another.

Misleading when spoken; leaving room for added doubles.

The mixture of galvanize emotions stirred up to gain one's trust, With the original intent falsified never once being discussed.

Even the tone of your voice was a sound of deceit;

Having everything a conversation needed but grounds for integrity.

With the exaggerated sentiments that needed to be purged, but all I heard was a bunch of crosswords.

Some would called them lies, but what you said; you yourself believed; so, I can't say what you were hoping to achieve.

Because even your truth is bowdlerized with absurd altercation; eliminating hope of anyone believing you in any situation

Nevertheless, you have not been misheard,

I'm just done with the idiocy and all the crosswords.

ME LIKE IT OR NOT

 If you have a problem with what you see

Let me tell you a few things and keep it short and sweet.

My hips are wide, too wide for some liking.

I'm tall... taller than most and still I'm striking.

The female soft voice for me doesn't exist.

But I'm still a bad mamma jammer handling my business.

NEGATIVE RESOURCES

Video cameras
Multiple eyewitnesses
World Wide News
Personal testimonies and interviews
Leave of absence while awaiting court hearings
Laws that governs our abuse and vindicate killings

Footage that's edited, missing or just down right ignored.
Onlookers are omitted, discredited or explored.
The whole world is aware that we're on some Hitler ish.
Allowing law enforcers to abuse and kill and the system justify it.

So how do I get your attention, when killing a black man is the norm?
Society clearly sees what's happening yet nothing is being done.

You're moving too slow.
While we're dying too fast

We can't walk to the store.
We can't knock on a door.
We can't have a past.
We can't ask questions.
We can't have a certain look.

Can't have a pep in your walk.
We can't play our music too loud,
Or sound a certain way when we talk.

And you wonder why there is such distrust,
Because we are fighting for a county that is fighting us:
With invisible boundaries that prohibits certain race,
A known fact disregarded in our face.

There are resources
No question about that
But does it apply to one if he or she is black?
No doubt the resources are indeed in place,
But is it used differently according to one's race.
And when of course the resources are use,
Disregarded by those in authority are they excused?

Eyes have seen and ears have heard
It's been written on paper; it's been spoken in words.
It's been declared the standard and made the law;
I think our negative resources have a hidden clause.

WORLD HUNGER

World hunger don't have a specific geographical location.
You can't classify hunger as one situation.

People are starving in all walks of life,
Rich... poor... young... old
Each has a specific need when their story unfolds.

There are people hungry for love.
Hungry for revenge
Hungry for God
People hungry for another chance

They don't stand in lines with their hands out.
It's not always televised; not always talked about.

There's people that is hungry... starving for the truth
Starving for power
Starving for food
Starving to be loose

We look into their faces and we past them by.
We don't acknowledge they exist because we don't hear their cries.

There are people hungry for romance
Hungry to be heard
Hungry for justice

Hungry for a word
For something that will give them hope and assure them they are
not alone.
The guarantee that there is help and it won't be prolonged;

For they are starving for answers
They are hungry for something new
Starving for miracles
Each one awaiting a breakthrough

So world hunger is real
It's out there no matter where you go
And the rich are starving just as much as the poor.
Chances are someone is starving in your view
And the reality is, sometimes it's you.

DON'T GIVE UP

Life has corners
A place when your back is against a wall
No need to turn because there's no place to run.
But don't give up!
Life has potholes
You're doing good and then you fall
The more you move you sink
You had a clear point of view but you blink.
Don't give up!
Then there are walls
In unexpected places; there to keep you bound
Blocking your way
Preventing access to the other side and the only way through it,
Is to tear it down.
But don't give up!
There are also roads in life that would tear your life apart
That lead to places where you cry out to God, to avoid
A combination of turmoil
Long... draining... ruthless
Relentless on the heart
But don't give up!
These things happen
They come but they go, claiming to help us grow
Often, they take more than we are willing to give
Teaching us more than we wanted to know.
But don't give up!
Life can deplete our strength
Brutally taunt our sanity

Insult our faith
Obstruct our abilities
But don't give up!
Learn to survive
Every time you take a breath, you past a test
Every time you open your eyes you've stayed alive
Don't give up!

PARENTAL GUIDANCE

Attention to the parents who have a child or children to raise.
If you don't handle your responsibilities
You'll be standing over pre-mature graves
Speaking with your child behind bars
Searching for them in the streets
Throwing blow with them like the enemy
Afraid to close your eyes with them in the house to sleep

When did children start setting their own curfews?
Taking it upon themselves to drop out of school.
Fixing their mouths to abuse the freedom of speech,
And not having a second thought of them losing their teeth.

For some school is a joke
Carrying a weapon is the thing.
They strike and fight those in authority
They go to jail with no shame.

But parents we can't give up
For each child there is a solution
And when they have the nerve to object
Introduce them to retribution.

Time out for being afraid of your own child
Save them from themselves
And let them know the enemy is on the prowl
Mentally, emotionally, spiritually and physically
Seeking who he may destroy or devour

Stand your ground put proper fear in their hearts
Established moral values let them know there's a God.
Invest in their education
Take notice of everything from the books they read to their
health.
Don't just raise them til they're grown
Raise them to be adults that can take care of themselves.

Single parents need to be mindful of the traffic they allow to
come through
Spouses need to unite and come into agreement
On what the child can and cannot do
Parental guidance should be respected
By both them and their friends
To not set boundaries is a crime shame
And for a parent a dangerous sin

Parental guidance shouldn't be a choice
Because it's your greatest tool; it is your voice.

PRAYING WITH NO TIME TO WASTE

As I arise unto another day, to God be the glory!
May I overcome another sin, break asunder another barrier
Open another door, Forsake another bad habit.
Should there be any rocks thrown my way let them miss their
mark.
Give the angels over me the strength to do their part.
Any negative words spoken are already condemned.
Keep me in the right frame of mind;
Protect the activities of my limbs.
Let any ungodly plans plotted and enemy unseen be exposed.
Give authority over my weaknesses so that sin will be unable to
impose.
May sickness flee my presence and accidents forsake my path.
Guide me in what to do or say
Should I have to deal with the confrontation of wrath;
Trouble shall not steal my peace and materialistic things will not
define my joy.
Secure my foundation and my prosperity.
And let the spirit of fear be unemployed.
Give me eyes to see the traps the enemy has set
I will not become victim to those who would suppress, kill or
destroy.
And give me the ability to identify the adversary and recognize his
decoy.
May the praise of my mouth be to your glory and the life I live
exhibit your saving grace. I go forth now In Jesus Name. Not my
will but Thy will be done today. Amen

CONTROL SUBSTANCE

Having the danger of addiction, abuse, physical or mental harm
Often told when used wisely it actually work like a charm
Most people think it comes in a bottle
In the shape, fashion or form of a pill
But some of these substances are on the street
Easily accessible, with no warning label or seal

Often times addictive
Because it comes in the form of love
And the victims are often silent
Because they're in denial of the end results

The discomfort is more than less
It keeps you from performing your best
This control substance has a voice and a tune
It often invites death in the room

It has a host of side effect
Black and blue eyes
Choke holds
Broken bones
Lack of contact with family and friends
The absence of peace within your home
Will power exploited
Self-confidence deflated

You're no longer your own

All your rights are wrong
This control substance is found and many different homes.

Help is available
But most victims for years will object
Even children are subject
To the vile side-effects
The withdrawals are the worst
Like any substance
You must make up your mind first
Although there are certain things you should know
The most important one
Is that you should go

Put it down
Let it loose
You no longer have need for its use

TEACH ME HOW TO DANCE

I want to move
See how my body movement and music play
I want to strike a pose
Shut it down when I walk away
I want to own the story
To the lyric of the song
I want to pop, lock and drop
Dance to the music stop
I want to slide, swing and sway
Like I'm a dance-a-thon buffet

Teach me how to dance
Move with the blues
Rock with rock and roll
Bop with hip hop
Roll with soul

I hear the music
It's all in me
I just need the steps to take
To set my spirit free

My fingers are popping
My head is bopping
My hands clapping

And my feet tapping
Teach me how to dance!
I'm starting to feel like Cassius Clay
I'm going in the ring
I don't care what they play

And I don't care what they're saying
I don't care what they playing
I'm having a ball
As long as I don't fall
Tapping and swinging
Moving and grooving

Now that I've done all that I can!

Just teach me how to dance!

THE FACE OF HATE

A despicable characteristic that clings to a person heart
Without a conscience
Having no sensitivity...
Creating repulsive imaginations
That is just down right mean

Hate don't whisper or talk
It screams
To drown out positive proposition
Or sound reasoning
It smoothers anything that makes sense
Even when a solution to its darkness exist

Its complex demeanor
And its provoking approach
Infuriate the atmosphere of those it oppose
It eats alive the capsule in which it finds shelter
Until its victim is enthralled and don't know any better.

It exercise control as it corrupts the soul
Eliminating the desire for hope
Incapacitating one's ability to cope

HERE I STAND

Here I stand thank God that I can
To represent the lives and cries of young men
Time and time again we've stated they needed more knowledge
So we educate our young men and send them off to college
Others joined the Army, Navy, Air Force and Marines
To fight for a country that down play their very being.
A grown man kills a child and it's alright
Yet another man kills a dog and it's a fight.

Here I stand, thank God that I can
Cause I could be shot down because of the color of my skin
You got a right to kill, I have a right to live
Who gave you the right to the breath of life?
Now you're above God and the Human Rights?
The laws and government is often twisted to a black man demise
And those in authority choose to ignore our cries
But the day is coming when judgment will take place
And your lies and deceit will be written all over your face.
But until then I choose to stand bold and strong all in my black skin.
Cause the way I see it...I won't lose but I can't win.

But here I stand, thank God that I can
But still other chose to see me less than a man;
I have dreams and hope, of getting ahead
But the cold in heart rather see me dead.
Does it take a revolution to get your attention?

Cause we're running out of time and there'll be no extension.
A life here today can be gone tomorrow
And once a brother gone it's not like life can be borrowed;

Even at his best, it's like a failed test.
Obama the first black president and half the nation in distress;
Now every white man isn't wrong and every black man isn't right
But we still have some issue that's worth the fight.
So I can't hold my peace and I will take a stand
All in my bold black skin

You say I'm angry
Yes, I'm still angry and I have a right to be
When I'm looking at you but you're looking down at me.
I'm nobody's fool I can read between the lines.
Attempted murder you're guilty.
Succeed to kill you're fine.
So they summon our lives with words unsaid

With hung juries and mistrials

Enslaving us to injustice in a modern day style;

There's no rope around our necks and there's no sheet on your
heads

But everything in the law points to leaving us for dead.

I might not have seen a man hung from a tree,

But it's not nothing to see him shot down in the street.

The law can shoot an unarmed man 41 times and no one wants to
admit that it was a crime.

Drag by a truck until his body can no longer be identified,

Not to mention, shady towns lies and cover up, for a black man is
no surprise.

Killed while going out for a bag of candy

Shot cause his music too loud
Because some fool wants to push a gun law to kill, called Stand
Your Grounds.
So if a racist attempts to kill us, he gets time
But if he leaves us dead he gets off with the crime.

Nonetheless, here I stand, thank God that I can
And I don't apologize for it for any man.
This injustice is writing out a prescription for the wrong lesson to be learned
Because you're sending out a message for the table to turn
Do what you might, say what you will,
Just make sure you're not writing a prescription too strong to fulfill.

OUR MAN POWER

A symbol of purpose
You're our family breastplate.
The backbone of legends
A monument of our race;

You are the beacon of our future
A treasure among men
We honor you with our hearts
We gratefully give you our hand.

Your voice is the sound we await
At the beginning and ending of each day;
When we think of noble men, knights and kings
It's you our minds portray.

When you were broken
Given less than a chance
We still saw your strength
In spite of your circumstance;
And though your tears were private...
Your cries were heard
We understood your position
Without you saying a word;
Now time has allow us to recognize your trace
Your presence... Your contribution... Your essence to the human race;
Be encouraged as you stand,

In your position to lead;
Immerse in your purpose
That we may follow in the sketches of your dreams.
For you our grandfather's
Our father's... our uncles...brothers... grandsons and sons.
We salute to you due admiration
For a job well done

YOU DO THE MATH

If every time you look around, there is more to your problem;
You've done nothing but subtract and it is still getting larger.
Check the calculations for some hidden exponents.
Stop what you're doing and check your circumference.

You know when you add one and one you get two.
If you get anything higher
Simply put... go back to school.

Now it could be you might want to check the square root.
Because you should always know what you're working with,
When you're looking for the truth;

Multiplication will only increase your sum
But you're not ready if you're still trying to add one plus one.
So nine times out of ten; Ready or not...
It sounds like you may have to divide...
Based on experiences and stories told,
This usually happens when you're dealing with lies.

Just when you think you have a common denominator
An absolute value to your core;
Here comes a cross-product with a factor that doesn't help your
score.

Arithmetic is not as complicated as some make it seem;

Instead, it's the mixture of geometric chemistry
That fails to runs parallel, due to unidentified schemes.

So do your homework
And get a tutor if need be;
Because anybody knows one plus one isn't three.

LAY-AWAY TROUBLE

It doesn't make sense, because you don't think it shows;
That it doesn't add up and certain ones already know;
Your game of innocent, as quiet as it's kept,
Is more than obvious
A certified bounce check;

You play your role
And all others involve
Pretending neither of you knows
Each one is playing their part.

Then when the "ish" goes down
And you just happen to mess up;
You expect me to believe
It was a stroke of bad luck.

So since you want to role play
Let's just see who will have the last say.

I'm not for this game of "Just in case I need to"
Because it's no more than trouble
You're lining up to do, when it's convenient for you.
But since you seem to play with fire
And still think everything will be fine;
I don't want to hear the lame excuses
When you just happen to cross the line;

And did I mention?
Lay-away trouble presents other issues too,
So keep your eyes open,
Because the other issues applies to you;
Something to think about
When you want something new;

You're *not* slick but go ahead and slide.
Take your time and enjoy the ride.

Cause I never told you, how I like shopping
And cash and credit cards aren't always what's dropping.

I have other means of getting what I want too.
That lay-away policy...
Don't just work for you.

TRAINED EMOTIONS

Anytime you can manipulate your tears
Tell a lie and make it sound real
Pretend to be something you're not
Control the whole situation with the right plot.
React to the surroundings and cause a scene
Do the crime and come out clean;
You're about that business you have your own enterprise,
That consists of trained emotions fit for living a lie.

THE BREAK IN

With the entry ways secured and the alarm set
I don't recall putting my guards down due to open threats.
I had locks with keys… bolts… and combinations
Had anyone even come close to entering,
They would have met unforeseen limitations.
I had sealed any openings due to cracks
Strengthen weaken foundations and posted warning signs
Both out front and back;
For me prevention was the solution
To eliminate the unwanted pollutions,
That spoiled images of hope and falsified love restitutions.
It's a wonder anyone got in
Because my doors and walls, they blend
But …
I'll call him Superman
He declared I had a host of violations
And he immediately went in on the renovations.
Tearing down years of hardcore structure
And rebuilding with a steadfast tender texture;
I often wonder how he ever made it in,
My alarm never went off and I never saw him coming.
He's here now and I don't want him to leave,
And I refuse to press charges against a worthy thief.

LORD YOU ARE

You have been more faithful than the beat of my heart
You are deeper than the color of my skin
You've been more consistence than time itself, and far more
amazing than any event.
You're stronger than any force,
Be it known to man
You're more powerful than any drug or nation
You're more loyal than any friend.
You are more awesome than any discovery,
You're mightier than any vessel of power.
You're steadfast in your position...
Every second, every minute, every hour.
You're a picture without flaws
A husband that won't stray
The gift we'll forever open
You are He who will have the last say.
You are more dedicated than any vow, constitution, or law,
You are God and you are God above All.

GOD STILL IS

No matter the status a person may hold;
God is still God and He's still in control.
Times are forever changing and people come and go.
Geographical locations have been destroyed by catastrophes and often times wars.
Creations are being made, while discoveries are being found.
Yet God is still God forever more; beyond the heavens, having no bounds.
Laws have been made and governments established.
There are many powerful forces; many profound dynamics.
There is the speed of sound and the awesome magnitude of light;
Nevertheless, God is still God enclosed with all glory, all dominion and all might.
(Now everybody say AMEN)

ADULTERY

Adultery at its best is still a hot mess
Rings that once represented love are no longer tokens
When vows are secretly being broken
Lies becomes the norm; creating a storm
Dress in the darkness of betrayal; causing the marriage to derail
For selfish lust blinds common sense
What was once a unified goal become past tense.
The psychological games, trivia's and tricks
And the exhaustion from the negative energy forms a risk
Long after the fidelity stops
Because one thought entertaining the exchange of love for
betrayal worth the swap.
Now there's one spouse harboring a question secretly
"Do I really know the person in front of me?"
With trust broken, memories of deceit and the echo of lies
Truth be told, many have tried to recuperate afterwards
But only the strong survive.
Adultery is like standing in the way of a bullet
It's a marriage Russian roulette
One or two bullets might miss you, but you're bound to get hit.

LETTER TO A PEDOPHILE

You were everything a woman wanted and everything a man thought he wanted to be;

But to the little girls and boys who knew you;

You were nothing less than a beast.

Wearing the titles "a godly man", "next to kin" or "outstanding friend"

 Was all a part of your plan for your forbidden sins

You had the character of evil at its worst

Acting like the devil tool he used to rehearse.

You've created places where secrets begin

You know where the truth starts, and you know where it ends

A rated X scary movie among us that had been released,
With hands that was able to reach beyond its screen
Subjecting your viewers to its horrific scenes

The lights didn't have to go out for fear to enter the room, just the thought of being left with you alone had its own gloom.

But as time went on you left a trail

That brought your victims together, each one with their own story to tell
Cocktails of flashbacks, drugs, trained emotions and quiet storms

Gather backstage in the darkness of our soul, ready to perform

Because now we walk around dealing with derange thoughts of revenge
So, we continue to pretend
As if nothing happen or the situation never exist
Yet waiting on you to make the wrong move for us to recompence
Waiting for you to acknowledge your wrong or for a sign that you've changed
Because the orchestra of the past keep playing out the pain

You can't erase your wrong
Or ever justify what you've done
You're an old man now and it's unbelievable
Time has not healed all the wounds

To digest seeing others embrace you as you hide from the truth
Give me anxiety because I know the real you
And you know the real me
Now when you go to bed
You must have one eye open when you sleep
Your dreams are not the same
As for peace you've been rob
Because you now await the wrath of your victims
Or the judgement of God

ABOUT THE AUTHOR

Michelle Robertson is the author of a collection of short stories called *DEATH HAS NO RULES*, and the book *YOU SAY THAT TO SAY WHAT Food for Thought* a collaboration of original wise sayings. She is also the author of a number of plays including the *Masquerade of Adultery. Mrs. Robertson lives in North Carolina but spends a great deal of her time in New York and South Carolina where she stays actively involves in various projects. Because writing is her passion she is also at work on her first novel, so look for her on social medias and sign up to be one of the first to be informed of her future projects.*

Thank you for your support.

THIS MAY BE YOUR LAST CHANCE

His Hands

Compromise and silent years of tears

Procrastinating to avoid dealing with the fears

The bearing thoughts of mental strong holds and mindsets,

It's your life in his hands I need you to project.

His hands have become like fire

And his words enhance its flames

His eyes mirror their danger

While your eyes mirror their pain.

His hands that you entrusted to make you feel loved and secure,

Promotes wounds of agony in which he expects you to endure.

Crushed at the very presence of him:

His footsteps…

His smell…

His voice…

This man…His…His hands…His hands Wake up! Wake up Baby Girl!
He dag near killed you again.

Listen, registration is not required for you to take a stand.
And you can no longer seek mercy from this man's hands.

For they have formed as a weapon against you that could one day put you six feet under,

But what God has put together (That's you Baby Girl) let no man put asunder.

Manage your emotions; make a decision to restore your health,

The battle with this brother belongs to the Lord, you need to save yourself.

Should we partake to a phone call or maybe even a news flash,

To find that you're no longer in the land of the living and now we got this battle of un-forgiveness!

And what is there to be said if you're unable to recuperate,

Lord have mercy should your help come too late.

Wake Up! Wake Up!

From the captivity of his hands

Wake Up! Wake Up!

This may be your last chance.
Wake up! Wake Up!

My daughter...My sister.... My mother...My friend.

This story is dedicated to individuals of domestic violence. I write it in memory of different loved ones in mind that are no longer here with us today. I speak out NOT against the abusers, but against the powerful excuses that hold one bound to an unsafe relationship.

What if the victims of domestic violence could share with you the ugly truth from the grave?

That's right.

The grave.

A place where there is no return. No getting out this time. No waking up to the truth. Past the point of letting go and letting God; it's a place where the deepest of fears cast out its aftermath and the most triumphant warnings echo defeat.

Domestic violence is a type of Russian roulette where the participants are taking potentially lethal chances with situations that could cause one his or her life, and in some cases, the lives of innocent loved ones caught in between the rage.

Of course, there are those who live through the experience of it all and live to tell about it. They live with the memories, the physical scars, and often times some form of deformity due to extreme situations. Because it is often tolerated in the name of love, for some, domestic violence is an unveiled, well designed masked suicide. I ask again, "What if the victims of domestic violence could share with you from the grave, the ultimate warning. What do you think you would hear?"

I want you to listen close because those are the ones we will hear from.

(The Story)

Some place, I'm not exactly sure where, stood the spirit of ten women. They waited, hesitating to join hundreds of others who had arrived before them. Each one looking in dismay at the other, understanding without saying a word why they were all there. Almost in unison they became aware of the sounds of acquainted voices coming from afar. Looking amiss and dismayed, each woman forgetting one another, immediately tried to provide answers of comfort to their loved one's questions and bitter wails of agony. While distant and faint in volume, each voice was recognizable no matter how many were being heard. As if pleading, wailing, and even venting hopelessly, the familiar sounds struck a wave of response from each woman.

Unbeknownst to them, they had joined the hundreds of women who had arrived before them and another ten, maybe even fifteen, now stood where they had previously resided.

Why I'm here I really don't know but since I'm here, let me tell you what I see:

The women are moving forward into a space that is beyond my ability to see where to. Their bodies seem to be translucent through the clothing and what I see is almost unbelievable... women with bruises, wounds and scars that mirror their exit from life.

If this is what one calls a stroke of love, then tell me what love has to do with it.

Who needs love that cuts into one's flesh so deep it penetrates the organs?

Or who wants to carry around engaged bullets and foreign objects in wounds too deep to close?

What kind of love burns one's flesh or strikes one so hard that it becomes the stroke of death?

When did love start leaving one's eyes black and blue or shut never to reopen?

How can one love you that literally, take your breath away?

The questions wouldn't stop coming and the answers couldn't be heard. I couldn't take it anymore. I had to have some answers. I grabbed the hand of an older woman hoping to find an answer with wisdom and a sense of knowledge to the madness. But when she turned, I saw she had been severely ill. Residue from the gurgitation of chemicals or perhaps an overdose of medication, resided from the corner of her mouth down the front of her.

It took all I had but I asked, "Ms. what happened?"

With tears in her eyes she answered, "The love of money, that's what happened. Twenty-seven years and his love for money has always been more than his love for me." She wiped at her mouth and with the tears now streaming down her face she pleaded with me, "Don't you come here child! Trust me when I tell you.

No movie, song, or story can describe or duplicate the tormented cries of one's children, the agony of a mother or the anguish of a father. No one is able to give an account for the sleepless nights or the stolen tomorrows, your loved ones will have to face. When you leave like this you might as well leave them with a broken piece of glass because no matter how they hold it, they'll never be able to grasp this domestic violence thing tight enough to make any sense out of it. You know why?" Without even giving me a chance to respond she continued in bewilderment, as if she were still in disbelief about her disposition. "Because it's senseless... Just down right senseless! If I had to do it all again I wouldn't lie to myself. I wouldn't make excuses for ignoring the warning signs. I wouldn't tell myself since nothing has happened in all this time, nothing will happen. I would spare my loved ones the pain and agony of dealing with my death on such a crucial level. I would believe more in myself and I would make it without him one way or another."

Though I wanted to say something, I was speechless. Domestic violence certainly did not discriminate. Like some people believe you don't die young, a part of me had always believed that my elders were exempt from this woe.

I remained alert while focusing on the different ages and ethnic groups. What caught me off guard was a young man who looked to be in his early thirties, medium build, with a nasty wound of some sort to the head. He abruptly pushed past several women, looking over each as if he were searching for a particular familiar face.

The echo of a woman crying out for her children startled me and I lost sight of the young man. I quickly turned around and found myself face to face with a young woman whom wept bitterly. She appeared to be in her early to mid-twenties. Whips around her neck, black and blue eyes, and multiple bruises covered what might have been the face of a once lovely woman. I must have appeared to be able to offer her some form of comfort, because she took the liberty of sharing with me her thoughts. "My children depended on me to protect them. Huh, I might as well had pulled the trigger and shot them myself. Holding on, to a man that couldn't love himself let alone anyone else. My biggest warning was fear. I remember having so many fears concerning him. Fear of him losing control and hurting me... fear of my losing control and hurting him before he could hurt me... fear of threats made by him, fear of ticking him off... fear of this... fear of that... just a constant sense of fear more than not. As if his words and physical abuse didn't do enough damage, this man has killed my children. I wasn't supposed to die. Oh no! I was supposed to live and suffer for the sake of not taking him seriously. It would have been just another one of his ways, by all means, of controlling me." Suddenly she stopped weeping, took a deep breath, and stated her claim. "Without my children I would have been an empty shell and I couldn't live like that. The wounds in my mind and in my heart held more pain than my physical body ever felt. Tomorrow without my children seemed like too much. So, I spit on him knowing death would follow. He choked and cursed me at the same time and suddenly as if he came up with this brilliant idea, he just stopped. His exact words were "-itch" I want you to live and feel the pain." I felt my heart flutter and parts of my body swelling from the furious blows he had inflicted upon me. I felt the loss of my bladder and a violent jerk that was followed by a vicious shake. At some point during the confrontation my brother and a friend had arrived at the scene. Within moments, I went from being in the hands of my violent lover to the hands of my desperate brother who screamed at the top of his lungs, "Hold on, I got you, I'm here, I got you!" I heard a scream, some sirens, a struggle of commotion of some sort, followed by more screams and official sounding voices. In the mist of it all, I slipped out. Without fighting for another breath, I went from life into death."

In tears, I turned away knowing there were no words of comfort I could now offer to the young woman. There is no turning back the hands of time and what was done had most definitely taken its toll. Death looked more inviting than living without her children. The thoughts of dealing with the possibilities of ridicule and judgment, of those she would have to answer to and live among from day to day, was overwhelming.

So somewhere in the land of the living, apart from her abuser, the condemnation of her loved one's judgment prevailed over their love and support. Even in death the lashing of their bitter grief echoed blame and misunderstanding.

The young man with the ghastly wound appeared again but this time he demonstrated a more aggressive demeanor in his pursuit. His focus was clearly on one woman. She also noticed him and immediately, as if overcome with fear, she dropped to her knees holding herself tightly and prepared for his approach. A warm rage came over me and without thinking twice I headed in their direction to her defense. I was less than twelve feet away from her but in his fury, he'd reached her before I did. My feeble attempt to protect her was brought to a halt when the young man spoke. His words were like a glaze of admonition filled with the anguish of hopelessness. She held her head down in shame, forcing herself to look up at him.

"Why did you do this to me?"

"Huh" was all she muttered.

"What part of, "It's over!" didn't you understand?" He yelled while examining her for an answer. "Ending my life for the sake of venting is irreversible. I don't deserve this!" Reaching for her arm, he gasped. "No not a murder, suicide! Patricia you didn't!"

In a feeble attempt to speak again, she managed an, "I'm-"

"I'm what? I'm sorry! Hell, Patricia, I'm sorry! I'm sorry I didn't leave a long time ago. How many men would allow a woman to batter and continually insult them on a regular basis? Your temper and outrage have cost me my life! Now our sons don't have a father or a mother!"

"But-"

"But what? I'm your husband?"

"Pat, that's not a reason for me to have stayed. I know that now. It didn't give you the right to constantly criticize or trample over my self-esteem and self-worth as an individual. It dag sure did not give you the right to end my life or compromise our son's future by excluding them the benefits of having either one of their parents."

Although he was angry you could still hear the disappointment and emotional hurt that was caused by his dilemma.

The young lady stood to face him but didn't speak. She trembled as she took his hand and kissed it while tears streamed down her face.

"I saw the signs. I heard the warnings," spoke the young man with more bewilderment than any other emotion. "I just ignored them as if they didn't apply to me. My mother, the preacher, even my best friend, all prayed and counseled me as best they could. They all spoke of their concerns for my safety and well-being. From the outside looking in they could see something was not right. My mother often worried about her grandchildren. Even more so, she felt you could possibly commit suicide. I should've listened,"

"But listen."

"No, you listen Patricia," he actually spoke with compassion for the young lady now kneeling before him and weeping. "I didn't hear them before, but I can sure hear them now; their cries, their moans of anguish, and the constant replay of how they had tried to warn me. I hear, and I can see clearly now what I had refused to acknowledge and deal with for years."

As she held tightly to his hand, he gently pulled her to her feet. The two stood there together for a moment, as if listening for a verdict to be read.

He pulled back his hand to walk away and she pleaded, "Listen! Pleaseee!"

"I am listening Pat. I hear my mother, I hear my children. I hear the now deflated warnings."

And just as suddenly as he'd come, he was gone, lost within the crowd that continued to move forth steadily.

I asked God to forgive me for passing judgment on the couple so fast without knowing the full story. I had immediately thought he was the abuser.

Huh, I think I'm in for a rude awakening.

One thing I'm sure of based on all I saw so far is that every person needs to think about where they are in life right now. Think about the people you allow yourself to be entangled with. How and with whom you spend your time. Be true to yourself about your situation and please don't lie to yourself of all people. What do you tell yourself about the things you believe and are your beliefs the truth or a lie? Now ask yourself, "Does anything in my lifestyle or decision-making hurt who I am or present any toxic repercussions?"

I should leave now but the crowd keeps coming. I'll stay a little bit longer then I'm out of here.

A rather large woman to my left is looking around immobile as if she refuses to follow the crowd. I know if she turns to face me, the full view of her body will expose an ungodly image; an image that would serve as a witness to her demise. Holding herself tightly she slowly turned in my direction as I somehow knew she would. Lord have mercy, it appears she's been in a terrible accident. The bruises on her face alone were whelps of swollen flesh that had risen to the occasion. I realized then that she was moving as best as she could, against the agony of her swollen and pain-stricken body.

I reach out to touch her, to assist her somehow and was taken aback by her sigh to my touch. "Please don't touch me. Please just don't touch me." With blood shot eyes she looked at me as if she'd seen a ghost. "Do you know what it's like to be beaten to death? Punched, hit, stomped, and even spit on. Do you know how it feels to get hit so hard you hear your bones break and feel your flesh rip apart from the inside? You don't know that someone can really knock the mess out of you and leave you urinating blood instead of urine. Lady, I've been beat so bad that I've been unconscious for hours at a time, but I survived more than most. My mother was just punched in the stomach by my father and suffered a heart attack. She died before they could get her to the hospital. I was eight years old and saw everything. Nobody ever knew what caused her heart attack but my dad, the good Lord and I. As she lay gasping for breath he franticly realized what he'd done and the situation he'd now found himself in. Two hours later when he learned that my mother had passed away, he cried for what seemed like years. In my young mind it was an accident because he cried so hard and for so long. That did something to me. I thought I was strong because I had survived my lover's physical abuse and figured I'd take it until I couldn't take it anymore. He must have had the same intentions in mind because this time he beat me until he got tired and my soul gave up. I don't know which one came first but it came and I'm here. Hurting from the inside out and wishing someone would find my body so I can finally rest in peace."

I gasped, "What are you saying? Nobody knows you're gone?"

"No. Nobody knows. They have their suspicions that he's done something and is searching with hopes that I didn't stay too long. It's amazing how everybody saw it coming, but me. Hon, do yourself a favor and listen by learning from others' mistakes sometimes. No need for everybody to go through the same thing. Be real and true to thyself. Love you. Loving you is a form of love that is just as real as any other love. Listen to that inner voice that warns you when something is wrong. Wake up. Don't sleep on it."

I'm was still paralyzed by the fact that she'd been murdered, and no one knew.

I ask, "Where are you? I mean where can they find you?"

"I'm under my house. I was too heavy for him to take me much farther. I can hear the dogs barking and they are really close. I hear footsteps of someone going back and forth. It's him walking over my dead body and I refuse to let him rest. My voice will be heard even from the grave, no matter where I lie. You must wake up, you hear? Wake up!"

Her lurid expression startled me, and I had to regain my composure after having backed up against a young child. Disregarding her command, I turned to acknowledge the small frame by reaching to embrace him. This was no place for a child. For a moment the antics of this place seemed inappropriate for someone his age, until I took a good look at him.

He looked up at me with a smile on his face that strangely resembled the one on his neck.

"Are you an angel?" he asked.

"No baby," I answered, trying to figure out his age. "How old are you?"

"Four!" He smiled hard, "I just had a birthday."

I took a deep breath and observed the innocent face of this child who too had become a victim of a domestic situation.

"Tell my mama to stop crying. I'm okay."

"What?"

"Her boyfriend Patrick cut my throat. He's all the time hurting me, but not no more."

"Didn't you tell your mother?"

"I did, and she fussed him out, but he wasn't scared of her. One time he put the knife to her throat too. That made her real mad and she put him out the house for a long time. When he came back, he was really nice to us for a while, but then he got mean again, especially when he would drink."

For lack of a better response I replied, "I am so sorry baby." He must have sense I didn't know what else to say.

"You sound like my mama. That's what she'd always said. "I'm so sorry baby." I hear her now. She's always sorry for what Patrick has done to me."

"Who exactly is Patrick?" I asked, already having my own conclusion as to who he was.

"I told you. Patrick is my mama's boyfriend. I used to like him cause he used to help my mama pay the bills and buy us nice things."

I was speechless at how he talked about his abuse and abuser as if it were all normal. His little spirit seemed to be untouched by the unfamiliar atmosphere and its surroundings.

He continued, "I just got here. Mama was crying and said I was going to a better place. She didn't really want me to go but she said for me to go ahead she'll be coming soon one day. She told me to look for Jesus. That he'd be waiting, and there'll be no more pain or troubles, and no more people like Patrick to hurt me."

His little soul was filled with so much faith, he left without any farewell. He went ahead amongst the mixture of souls that were both young and old. The majority of them were women but there were men and even children. His appearance faded right before my eyes as he was approaching the multitude.

The heavy-set woman had remained in place as if she were waiting to finish our conversation. "Wake up! Wake up I said! What are you waiting for?"

It was then that I felt the blow to my abdomen and I could taste and smell blood. My head spun, and I was back and forth from one extreme to another.

Was I here or was I there?

No doubt I was here, somewhere real that was connected to a hemisphere in the spiritual world. I was standing here but I could see there.

I saw myself ball up into a fetal position in a pool of blood. In my right hand was a registered weapon given to me by my brother several months earlier. In my left hand was my dismantled home phone. I recognized the voice of the medical emergency team by the questions they were asking and the professional verbal approach. Then I heard a familiar voice pleading and begging for a response, "Wake up Casey! Wake Up!"

It was my brother and he was pacing the floor from one end of the room to the other. It was then the view of a body, other than my own appeared lying on the floor also surrounded by blood and medical professionals.

"Casey don't give up! Hold on sis, we're right here!" The pain in his voice came from a place deep down in the soul of a man.

I stepped closer to my body. The first step allowed me a clearer view, as to what was happening. I took another step closer and this time the memory of events that had led up to this moment swept in like the aftermath of a storm. Looking around I frantically searched for my attacker; my soon to be ex-husband.

Just hours earlier, he had phoned in saying we needed to talk. I had made it clear that there was nothing else for us to talk about. Our marriage was over and all I wanted was for us to come to an agreement concerning our children and our marital assets. He'd insisted on speaking with me face to face and had intentionally ignored the order of protection I'd had served on him. When he pulled up into the driveway of our home, I could see the look on his face through his windshield. I had come to know that look all too well. I shook my head, thinking this was once a man I loved. How he'd once been someone I use to share my dreams, my life, and my bed with.

How had I missed the warning signs?

Had they been there all along or had they developed at some point during our relationship?

Why was he consumed with so much anger and why was I his target?

Even as he sat in the car, the vision held me captive in a state of fear that left me feeling like my time here wasn't going to be long.

Here I was with two college degrees but no idea how this had happened. In the past he had made it clear he didn't want a divorce, but his actions had said otherwise. He'd started acting strangely and saying things that were signs of his violent behavior possibly escalating to a deeper level of danger. His anger became more obvious and I became more aware of something being terribly wrong.

When he got out the car, I didn't know what to do first; grab the phone or the gun. The locks had been changed so he had to knock in order to get in; at least that's what I thought. That would have been a reasonable idea had I not been dealing with an irrational individual. The truth set in when I heard the first shot.

"Oh my God! Oh my God! I can't believe it's going to lead to this! He's going to try to kill me!" I shouted in fear.

I grabbed the phone as I ran into the closet where I kept an already loaded 48 magnum. My heart was beating with the force of a drum. I was shaking out of control and perspiration lined my hairline. I proceeded to run out of my bedroom and into the hallway in an attempt to exit out the back door. All the while my life was flashing before me in slow motion. Midway to the door the second shot rang out and I felt as if a bolt of lightning had struck me. The phone fell to the floor as I dropped to my knees. In agony I stood back up, turning to face my biggest fear.

He was saying something with the gun still pointed at me. He seemed to be oblivious that the house alarm had been triggered and the message "the local police are on the way" was being repeated. It had no effect on my intruder. The mixed emotions of fear, anger, survival, and life without me flooded my conscious. Within seconds I decided my children would not come home from school to find their mother dead and I refused to let this man walk away with my life in his hands. I decided, I'll kill or be killed and that I had no other choice.

The fireworks went off and we went down in unison. I went numb. Reaching for the phone that had fallen within arm's reach, I continued to struggle to stay conscience. I could hear him gasping for breath as I struggled for my own. Not wanting to acknowledge what I was seeing, I felt the warm blood that was surrounding my body and blacked out before I could dial out for help.

My body was weak, but my soul was determined and the struggle between the two began. A part of me, my flesh, was tired and wanted to give up, but there was also a part of me that was determined not to become hostage to the ultimate rest. It was as if I had a choice to live or die.

Excerpt from the book, DEATH HAS NO RULES.

Available on Amazon

Made in the USA
Columbia, SC
23 April 2024

34498006R00065